THE CONSOLIDATED GOSPEL

JOHN SULLIVAN

CONTENTS

THE CONSOLIDATED GOSPEL

FOREWORD

God's Word as told through many scriptures continues to be forever eternal. There is nothing more beautiful yet amazingly simplistic in its complexity than the soul sustaining nourishment of God's Word. God's Word is infallible. It is the basis of all great achievements known to man and remains its sole source and power. The author(s) believe in the eternal and restorative power of God's Word. The authors feel there can be nothing added to or subtracted from God's Word that will beautify or marginalize the word in any shape, form or fashion.

- Always carry this little book with you and refer to it often throughout your day. The words within will provide the comfort sought that is reminiscent of companionship with GOD.

The authors hope the readers share this text with others as much and as often as they enjoy it and find peace within it.

Remember God's Promise

"I am with you always; I will not leave you or forsake you."

When you recognize GOD and begin working with Him,
GOD works with you.

- Faith is necessary and must first be established in
  your absolute belief in the Power of GOD and His
  promises.
- You must learn to love, praise and glorify your
  Father in Heaven, Be obedient and Be exceedingly
  thankful for all the blessings He bestows upon you.
  You will find GOD'S promises nourishment for
  the body and soul, and the supreme remedy for
  every need in your life.
- You will find GOD'S promises nourishment for
  the body and soul, and the supreme remedy for
  every need in your life.
- Turn to the page for your need, read it over
  carefully as often as you choose and repeat your

affirmation. Then Think, Act, and Live as this "Truth" directs you.

- By this constructive means you can create and mold the conditions in your life and Become Master of Yourself and Your Environment.

- You are given All Power to get the things you desire and should begin to understand how this Power serves you, when you acknowledge and work in harmony with it.

- As you grow in this higher consciousness, You Can transform your life into a prosperous and happy one and Be Victorious Over All Things.

Words are better understood if always spoken in kindness.

Think Right, Act Right; for it is what we think and do that makes us what we are.

"Be ye kind one to another, tender hearted; forgiving one another even as GOD has forgiven you." Ephs. 4: 33

"Pleasant words are like a honey-comb, sweet to the soul and health to the bones." Prov. 16: 24

<u>Affirmation</u>

Acts of kindness and forgiveness bring rich reward to the soul.

COURAGE

To be fearless, we need to develop a sense of courage in
Christ. We need to know that He abides within us as our
unfailing courage, that He makes us unafraid in all situations.
Nothing can frighten us when we are assured that the courage
of Christ prevails within our heart and in our life.

Have strong courage and put your trust in GOD'S mighty
power. He will be with you; He will not fail you or forsake
you.

True courage is cool and calm

Conscience in the soul is the root of all true courage.

**The Spirit of GOD within you is the courage that frees
you from all sense of fear.**

"Be strong and of good courage for the Lord thy GOD is with
thee whithersoever thou goes." Josh. 1: 9

"I will wait on the Lord and be of good courage and He will strengthen my heart." Psalms 27: 14

Affirmation

Knowing that GOD will remove all my difficulties, I fully trust Him and go forth with courage.

Get acquainted with your true self and find happiness. It is within your own soul. (A part of the Divine.) Store up a little more joy each day and share it with others. It reacts on the mind and body and makes life worthwhile.

The Spirit of GOD within you is your constant inspiration to be happy. You should always rejoice because this Divine power lives with you as your constant reminder to be joyful and in all situations.

Happiness is the natural and inevitable Destiny of man.

This world would be a paradise if everybody were happy and living to make others happy.

"He that giveth heed unto the word shall find good; and whoso trusteth in the Lord, happy is he." Prov. 16: 20

The universe is a mirror that reflects back to you what you

mentally send out to it. Give to the world the best that you have, and the best will come back to you.

Affirmation

I rejoice in the "Truth" and find happiness in serving and obeying GOD.

CONFIDENCE

Confidence in GOD gives us faith in Him and makes us
patient. We have no desire to try to hasten the work of GOD
when we know that He is active in us and in all our affairs.
We are content to rise out of personal striving and to wait
confidently for Him to cause our good to appear.

The patient person plainly shows that he has confidence in
GOD. The outside world may strive to vex and disturb him,
but its voice fails in luring him from his high consciousness of
trust and patience.

Never lose confidence in your real self, the DIVINE
POWER within you, Life, Intelligence, Soul.

"It is better to trust in the Lord, than to put confidence in
man."
Psalm 118: 8
Recognize the Spirit and it acts.

"Let the Lord be thy confidence; He will not suffer thy foot
to be taken." Prov. 3: 26

No person or circumstance can separate me from my perfect
union with the Spirit of all good. I have found union with
GOD; He is my Creator and I can never be separated
from Him.
"In quietness and confidence shall be your strength."
Isa.30: 15

**Divine power is now given to me to perform every
task.**

HEALTH

We can have perfect health and harmony in our lives, when we know and apply the laws governing the body, mind and spirit. All healing really comes from within.

The body is the temple of GOD and His presence fills it with life, health and strength. Knowing this truth, we free mind and body from all belief in disease and weakness. We remove from the body every trace of disease when we know the truth of GOD'S abiding presence.

Keep calm and serene and keep your heart filled with love and kindness toward every human being; this will cause the body to respond to the touch of Divine life working within you.

"The tongue of the wise is health." Prov. 12: 18

"I will serve the Lord and He will take all sickness away from me."
Ex. 23: 25

"I will prosper and be in health even as my soul prospers." III John 1: 2

"I will restore health unto thee, and I will heal thee of thy wounds saith the Lord." Jer. 30: 17

- **<u>Affirmation</u>**
- **GOD heals all my diseases and infirmities now, while I wait upon Him.**

PEACE

If you would be peaceful, turn every inharmonious thought into a peaceful one. Watch your thinking. Things of the world about you cannot give you peace. You must find this in the consciousness of GOD'S presence.

There is a tremendous power to be derived from identifying yourself with your indwelling Spirit. Here you will find infinite peace.

Realize that in Truth there is only GOD'S world of peace, in which you forever abide with Him.

"The fruit of the Spirit is LOVE, JOY, PEACE, LONG SUFFERING, KINDNESS, SELF-CONTROL." Gal. 6: 22

"And into whatever house ye enter first say: Peace be to this house." Luke 10: 15

"Acquaint now thyself with Him, and be at peace, thereby good shall come unto thee." Job 22: 21

"These things I have spoken unto you, that in Me ye may have peace. In the world ye have tribulation: but be of good cheer; I have overcome the world." John 16: 23

"But the meek shall inherit the earth and shall delight themselves in the abundance of peace." Ps. 37: 11

"Thou wilt keep him in perfect peace, whose mind is stayed on thee: because he trusteth in thee." Isa. 26: 3

AFFIRMATION

Peace flows like a river through my mind and I thank GOD that I am one with Him.

FAITH

Faith in GOD increases as we cease to pin our faith on other things and think exclusively of Him. We find that we no longer believe that any other presence or power can help us. We give up all doubt about GOD. We trust Him implicitly in all things.

Having faith in GOD during us is certain to give us faith in ourselves. We come to know that we can do all things through Him. We are inspired to have faith in our fellow man, to behold the good in him.

When you find yourself weak, your spirits low, and your prospects dreary, this is the very time to honor and obey GOD'S invitation.

"Look unto me."

I am saved from pain and sorrow through my faith in the care and protection of God.

"Faith is both the gift and the fruit of the Spirit."

"According to your faith be it unto you." Matt. 9: 29

Ask of GOD and you shall have the desire of your heart. Stretch out your hand by faith and receive it.

"Faith is the substance of the things hoped for." Hebrews 11: 1

Through our faith we draw blessings to us. Faith heals, prospers and never goes unrewarded.

To the degree of my faith in GOD, I am the possessor of all good things.

Affirmation
All unbelief leaves me as I increase my faith in GOD.

"Therefore, I say unto you, what things so ever ye desire, when you pray, believe that ye receive them, and ye shall have them." Mark 11: 24

LOVE

Love is unselfish. If we have the consciousness of
real love we have lost our selfishness.

Love is impersonal. The person who has the love of
GOD in his heart loses all inclination to focus love
upon a few individuals. True love cannot be limited to
the bounds of one family, or to the confines of a
limited sphere.

Love is universal. One who shares the universal love of
GOD is in love with all living things. The universe is
the field of his affection and in the universal love of
GOD he finds love for all persons and all things.

Love never takes advantage of others. Love
always considers the other person; his welfare comes
first. Love seems to thrive in doing good to others.

Love increases when another's happiness increases.

**Love is the key which opens the door to GOD'S
rich storehouse.**

**Love restores peace and harmony where
reasoning and every other method fails.**

**Keep your heart filled with love, for it is the
light and sunshine of life.**

"Thou shalt love the Lord thy GOD with all thy heart
and with all thy soul and with all thy mind; and thy
neighbor as thyself." Mt. 22: 37

"He that dwelleth in love dwelleth in GOD and GOD
in him." I John 4: 16
"All things work together for good to those that love
GOD." Rom. 8: 39

Love is **the greatest power in heaven and on earth.**
Love is infinite – its Spirit blesses all whom it reaches,
rests upon or touches.
<u>Affirmation</u>
**The love that I now send out to all my fellow men is
an expression of GOD'S love to me.**

WISDOM AND UNDERSTANDING

Wisdom is of GOD. His presence within us is the light of our understanding. He causes us to know whatever we need to know in order to live a full life and approach all situations through understanding and mastery. In Truth we are children of light. Until we know this truth, we may think of ourselves as ignorant or as living in the dark. The Spirit of wisdom within us quickens us to know whatever we need to know. We come to know ourselves as sons of GOD, children of His wisdom.

MAN IS NOT CREATED by GOD and then left without direction. Man ever carries with him the light of his Creator.

"The wisdom that is from above is first pure, then peaceable, gentle, easy to be entreated, full of mercy and good fruits, without doubtfulness, without hypocrisy." James 3: 17

"For to the man that please Him, GOD give wisdom, and knowledge, and joy." Eccl. 2: 26

"Understanding is a well-spring of life unto him that hath it." Prov. 16: 22

"He that hath knowledge spare his words; and a man of understanding is an excellent spirit." Prov. 17: 27

"Happy is the man that find wisdom, and the man that receive understanding: For the merchandise of it is better than the merchandise of silver, and the gain thereof than fine gold. She is more precious than rubies: and all the things thou canst desire are not to be compared unto her." Prov. 3: 13-14-15

"Wisdom is a tree of life to them that lay hold upon her." Prov. 3: 18

Affirmation

GOD now gives me understanding according to His perfect word.

FEAR NOT – TRUST AND BELIEVE

Many people go through life filled with fear. They do not seem to know just what they are afraid of, but they are so ruled by a subconscious fear that they shrink from the most harmless experiences in life. The consciousness of courage removes all sense of fear and causes us to see that there is nothing to make us afraid.

- The practical Christian has no occasion to worry. He is trained to trust GOD. Instead of being anxious about health, personal problems and business matters he gives himself and his affairs into GOD'S keeping and trusts GOD in all his ways.

Are you sitting today bowed down under your load of care?

**Turn to your Comforter, the Holy Spirit within
you, GOD.
"Call upon Me on the day of trouble: I will deliver
thee." Psalms 50: 15**

"Whoso hearkened unto Me shall dwell securely, and
shall be quiet without fear of evil." Prov. 1: 33

"Fear not I am with you always." Isa. 43: 5

"I will not leave you comfortless, I will come to you."
John 43: 5

**"GOD is my strength and power: and He make
my way perfect."
II Sam. 22: 33**

"The Lord is my light and my salvation, whom shall, I
fear? The Lord is the strength of my life; of whom
shall I be afraid?" Psalms 27: 1

"I shall cast my burden upon the Lord, and He will
sustain me."
Psalms 55: 22

**"I sought the Lord, and He heard me and
delivered me from all my fears." Psalms 34: 4**

**<u>Affirmation</u>
All worry and anxiety leave me as I put my whole trust
in GOD and all my affairs in His Hands.**

Today let us count over our blessings and see how many things we have for which we should be thankful. We should take into consideration the little things as well as those of larger proportions.

Has a need of yours been fulfilled today? Then just know that your soul's longing has caused you to look through eyes of faith and to behold GOD appearing as the fulfillment of your desire.

Being appreciative and grateful does a great deal for a person in helping to increase his blessings. The person who is grateful casts such an effect over his blessings that they seem to increase and to flourish.

Giving thanks for your blessings will cause you to see them manifest much sooner and in greater abundance than otherwise.

**We all know that it is GOD from whom all bless-
ings flow.**
**"And all these blessings shall come upon thee,
and overtake thee, if thou shalt hearken unto
the voice of the Lord thy GOD."**

"The blessing of Jehovah, it makes rich: toil add
nothing thereto." Prov. 10: 22

"If ye be willing and obedient ye shall eat the good of
the land." Isa. 1: 19
"Both riches and honor come of thee and thou reign
over all; and in thy hand is power and might." I Chron.
29: 12

**"Blessed shalt thou be in the city, and Blessed
shalt thou be in the field."**

Blessed shall be thy basket and thy store.

**Blessed shalt thou be when thou come in and
blessed shalt thou be when thou goes out.**

The Lord shall command the blessing upon thee in all
that thou set thine hand unto: and He shall bless thee
in the land which the Lord thy GOD giveth thee.

"The Lord shall open unto thee his good treasure, the
heaven to give the rain unto thy land in his season, and
to bless all the work of thine hand." Deut. 28: 3-5-6-8-12

**I continually give thanks to GOD Who is the
one source of all my blessings.**

SUPPLY AND ABUNDANCE

To acknowledge GOD and to depend entirely upon Him for
supply means that our source of prosperity is never limited
or depleted. He blesses and prospers us at every turn. If you
would be prosperous you must be established in the
consciousness of prosperity. Your mind must be filled with
prosperous ideas so that there may be no room for any
belief in lack. You must know for a certainty that your
Divine birthright is plenty, that the riches of your Father
are yours, that you have access to his storehouse of
substance.

**Never think of yourself as lacking supply. Do not have
any adverse or limiting thoughts about your business
or your work.** Bless it in the consciousness (**THE
UNIVERSE)** that prosperity is now being expressed in and
through it. **In GOD'S world there is no place for lack.
Lack cannot exist when you realize that GOD'S
substance is your supply.
You are entitled to all the good things that GOD has
put in this world for his children. Say, I belong to the**

kingdom of heaven, I am one of the family, and all the Father has is mine.
I look to my loving Father for all the good I am prospered.

"My GOD will supply all my needs according to his riches."
Ph. 4: 19
If ye abide in me, and my words abide in you, ye shall ask what ye will, and it shall be done unto you." John 15: 7

"Delight thyself in the Lord and He will give you the desires of your heart."
Psalm 37: 4

"Eye hath not seen, nor ear heard, neither has entered into the heart of man, the things which GOD hath prepared for them that love Him."
I Cor. 2: 9

"I shall eat in plenty and be satisfied; I shall praise the name of GOD who has dealt so wondrously with me." Joel 2: 26

"Those who obey and serve GOD shall spend their days in prosperity and their years in pleasures." Job 36: 11

"Thou shalt remember the Lord thy GOD: for it is he that giveth thee power to get wealth." Deut. 8

"It is your Father's good pleasure to give you the kingdom."
Luke 12: 32
<u>Affirmation</u>
The Divine hand makes my prosperous and I shall have success.

PROTECTION

Protection is assured when we meditate upon the presence of Christ and think of ourselves as one with it. **We see that fear, danger, disaster, and adversity cannot exist in Christ's (GOD'S) presence. WE ARE PROTECTED FROM EVERYTHING THAT WOULD SEEM TO ENDANGER OUR WELFARE AND WELL-BEING.**

Do you feel that the peace and love of GOD go with you wherever you go, protecting you from all that is inharmonious and unloving? Do you realize that you are saved many times a day from discomfort, inconvenience, and trouble because you have some of the consciousness **(GOD, THE UNIVERSE)** of protection that assures you of GOD'S presence, when in need?

Do you see that no harm can exist in your world when you live in the world of Truth? No danger can come to you when you know that your world is filled with GOD'S presence.

The Divine hand of God protects and covers me. I have survived everything I have encountered so fear is not of God therefore I shall not be afraid.

GOD

The Power Source

To create and attract to your life the things that you desire,
you must unite yourself with your

TRUE SOURCE OF POWER (GOD)

When you get understanding the Lord shall be unto you an
everlasting light.
To be abundantly supplied, keep your **Vision** toward the
Highest. (GOD).
Prayer brings you into direct contact with GOD and lifts
the burden from your heart.

**GOD will give you the Desire of your heart if you will
abide in Him and trust Him.**
Be of good cheer – **keep your thoughts, affections and
hopes toward**

**GOD. Trust the GOD Power within and act according
to its wisdom and guidance.**

The Divine Power of God alone is reason to have a cheerful heart. God is the source of all power. And as I choose to tap into that power, he has laid within me I draw closer to him and able to succeed, overcome and endure all I face.

I believe these timeless words of wisdom and inspiration will provide the reader with TRUTH, HEALTH, PEACE, HAPPINESS AND PROSPERITY.

To our family and friends, we hope this book has a positive impact on you and your life. The book has changed me. I believe it is making me a better man. I love you all.

MAY GOD, THE CREATOR, BLESS YOU, KEEP YOU AND GUIDE YOU ON YOUR JOURNEY!

UNTIL YOU ARE REUNITED WITH HIM TRAVEL WITH FEARLESS FAITH!